Contents

uYJ W
(ALL)
pamphlet

D195
460

1

Acknowledgements

Thanks to Carl Ward (AEWHA Director of Coaching) for collating and writing much of the information, and to Gill Clarke, John Gawley and Peter Brown for their contributions.

The publishers would like to thank Grays, Monarch and Puma for their photographic contributions to this book.

Photograph on the front cover courtesy of Allsport UK Ltd.
All other photographs courtesy of *Hockey Digest*.
Illustrations by Ron Dixon of Taurus Graphics.

Note Throughout the book players and officials are referred to individually as 'he'. This should, of course, be taken to mean 'he or she' where appropriate. All measurements are given in imperial units; a metric conversion table is given on page 47.

Introduction

Hockey is a very old game. There are records that a stick game similar to hockey was played by the Persians, Greeks and Romans. Modern hockey was introduced into England about 1875.

The Hockey Association was formed in 1886 and the All England Women's Hockey Association was established in 1895. The game remains one of the few purely amateur sports.

The game

Hockey is played between two teams of 11 players. A team may have only one goalkeeper on the pitch at any time; there is no other restriction on the formation adopted. Originally, all teams played with five forwards, supported by three halves and two backs, with the goalkeeper as the last line of defence. Gradually, however, other systems have evolved, leading to a variety of more flexible formations, with players usually classified simply as attackers, midfield players or defenders, and taking up positions worked out with the coach during training.

Another member of the team may change roles with the goalkeeper during the match, provided the umpire is notified. It is also courteous to notify the opposing captain if the change is made during half-time.

Up to five substitutes are normally permitted. They and the players they replace may interchange throughout the match under the control of the team captain or a delegated official at any time other than at a penalty corner or penalty stroke. Substitution at those times may take place, however, for an injured player.

The aim of the game is to score goals by sending the ball between the goal posts, the ball having been struck by the attacking team in the goal circle. The ball may only be hit with the stick, and may not be kicked, or thrown, or propelled by any part of the body.

The field

The size of the field can make a great deal of difference to the standard of play. If the field is too small the players will be crowded and good forward play and accurate movements from one player to another will be impossible. The *Rules of the Game of Hockey* states that the field should be 100 yds long and 60 yds wide, though for young players a small pitch is advocated, e.g. 55–60 yds long and 40–50 yds wide, when Mini or Junior 7-a-side hockey is being played.

Clubs should do their utmost to see that their fields are full size.

The surface of the field, if grass, should be kept level, close cut and well rolled. The marking should be 3 in wide, and all stones or other dangerous obstructions should be removed.

All-weather and artificial turf pitches are permissible: there is increasing use of these surfaces.

The centre line indicates the division of the field into two equal halves for the purpose of:

● pass-back – when all players except the striker must be in their own half of the field until the ball is in play
● penalty corner – when five of the defending team must be beyond the centre line until the ball is struck
● umpiring – each umpire has control of that half of the field which is on his right-hand side, when he is standing at the halfway line, facing the centre.

The side lines mark the width boundaries of the field. When the whole ball passes out of play over either of these side lines, a push-in or hit-in is taken by a player of the team opposed to that of

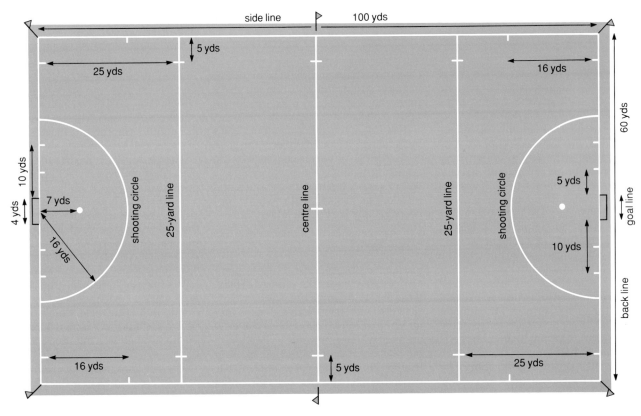

▲ *Fig. 1 Dimensions of the field*

the player who last touched it.

The back lines are the lines at each end of the field, joining and at right angles to the side lines.

The portion of the field in front of the goal mouth is called the 'goal line'. When the whole of the ball passes over the back or goal line, either on the ground or in the air, and a goal is not scored, the ball is out of play. The game is restarted by:

- a 16-yard hit-out – if the ball was last hit by an attacker or was last hit by a defender from a distance of 25 yds or more from the back line
- a push or hit from the back line within 5 yds of the corner flag – when, within the 25-yard area, the ball has been accidentally hit by the stick or glanced off the stick or body of a defender without an offence having been committed by that defender
- a penalty corner – if a defending player intentionally hits the ball over the back line from within the 25-yard area.

The goal line in front of the posts serves to show that when the whole of the ball has passed over the line, and under the cross-bar, a goal has been scored, unless otherwise provided for by the rules.

The goals

The goals are placed in the centre of each back line and behind each goal line, and consist of two perpendicular posts, 4 yds apart, joined together by a horizontal cross-bar, 7 ft from the ground. The two posts and the cross-bar should be 2 in wide and not more than 3 in deep. The sides of the posts and cross-bar which face the field should be flat, not curved.

Nets should be attached firmly to the goal posts and the cross-bar at intervals of not more than 6 in, and shall be attached firmly outside the back-board and side-boards.

Boards, 18 in in height, shall be placed at the foot of the goal net, the shorter boards being at right angles to the goal line. These boards should be painted a dark colour and should not project at the sides of the uprights.

The shooting circle

In front of each goal is a line 4 yds long, parallel to, and 16 yds from, the back line. This line is continued to meet the back line by two quarter circles, each with a goal post as centre. The space enclosed by these lines is the shooting circle. It serves the following purposes:

- indicates the area in which a forward may score a goal
- indicates the part of the field where the goalkeeper may kick the ball
- indicates the area outside which all attacking players (their sticks and feet), except the striker, must be when a penalty corner is being taken
- indicates that part of the field in which a penalty corner is awarded
- indicates that part of the field in which a penalty stroke may be awarded
- indicates the area into which the ball must not be lifted deliberately.

The 25-yard area

The 25-yard area is a rectangle 55–60 yds by 25 yds – i.e. the width of the field and 25 yds from the back lines.

5

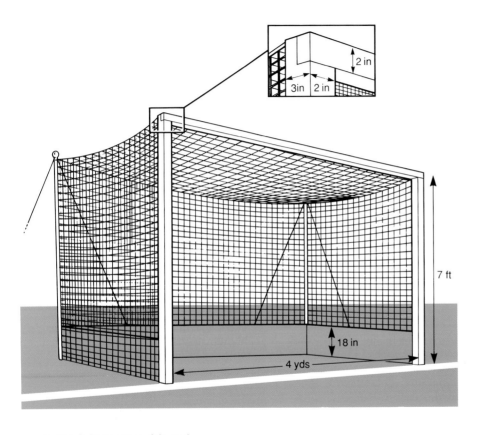

▲ *Fig. 2 Dimensions of the goal*

The 25-yard lines are unbroken right across the field. They serve the following purposes:

● to indicate that part of the field in which, if the ball glances off the stick or body of a defender over the back line, without an offence having been committed by that defender, or is hit unintentionally over the back line by a defender, a corner push or hit from the back line is awarded

● to indicate the area outside which all players must stand for a penalty stroke, except the two players taking part in it

● to indicate the area outside the circle in which a penalty corner may be awarded for an intentional foul by the defence

● to indicate the area in which a player can be offside.

The flag posts

Flag posts, at least 4 ft and not more than 5 ft high, are placed one at each corner, and one on each 25-yard line 1 yd outside the side line on the side opposite each umpire. They must not be removed during the game.

Equipment

Sticks

The head of a hockey stick should have a flat face on the left side, be made of uncracked and unsplintered wood, not more than 4 in long, and rounded at its tip, not squared off. It should be fitted to a handle of any suitable material (too many different materials to mention), which will usually have a non-slip covering.

The weight of a stick must not exceed 28 oz, nor be less than 12 oz. It must be thin enough for a ring of interior diameter 2 in to pass over the whole length.

The head of the stick must not have any insets, or fittings of hard wood or other substance, and sharp edges and splinters are not allowed. Surgical tape can be bound round the head to prevent splintering, providing the stick can be passed through a 2 in ring. On no account must the blade of the stick be cut square or be pointed, as this would make play dangerous.

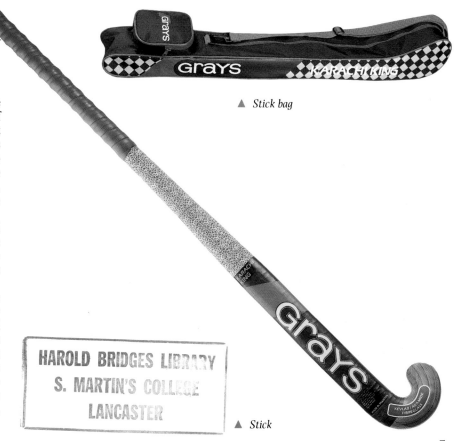

▲ Stick bag

▲ Stick

Ball

A ball of any material or colour, sewn or seamless, but of the correct weight and size, may be used as agreed mutually before the game. The weight should be 5.5–5.75 oz. The circumference of the ball should not be more than 9.25 in and not less than 8.81 in.

Uniform

To ensure that players are tidily and suitably dressed for the game:

● women shall wear skirts, shirts (the goalkeeper, however, is permitted to wear shorts or trousers) and knee-length socks
● men shall wear shorts and shirts
● cycling shorts with long legs, if worn as undergarments, shall be the same colour as the external shorts or skirt

▲ *Women's uniform*

Footwear

Shoes should have soles suitable for the playing surface, so it is advisable to find out before a match what kind of surface you will be playing on. Metal spikes, dangerous studs and protruding nails are prohibited.

◄ *Studded boots for grass surfaces*

- the size of shirt numbers and advertiser's logos shall conform with rules currently laid down by the appropriate association
- goalkeepers shall wear a colour different from that of their own team and that of their opponents
- the wearing of shin guards, knuckle/hand protectors and gum shields is recommended
- to prevent any possibility of injury, players must not wear metal badges or jewellery including ear-rings other than sleeper-rings.

Training shoes for artificial surfaces

The umpires

Umpires should carry:

● a current rule book
● a good whistle with a wrist cord
● two pencils
● a stop watch, or a reliable watch with a second hand
● a card on which to record the score
● a set of misconduct cards (*see* page 20).

The rules make no stipulation concerning the dress of umpires, but the following are recommended:

● suitable clothing allowing free movement
● shirts or jumpers should be of the same colour but different from those worn by either team and, if possible, the goalkeepers
● men should wear preferably grey trousers, and women grey or black skirts
● footwear should be similar to that of the players, appropriate to the playing surface
● a hat with a large peak to protect the eyes against rain or glare may be worn.

Goalkeeper's equipment

Goalkeepers may wear additional protective equipment, including special pads of high density foam (like cricket pads), kickers, gauntlets, body protectors (which must be worn under shirt or jacket), headgear, face masks and elbow pads. (*See* page 41 for a list of recommended equipment and for further information on goalkeeping.)

10

Rules of play

Duration of game

A game is divided into two periods of 35 minutes each, unless otherwise agreed before the game, with a half-time period after which the teams change ends. The interval should be normally five minutes, though no longer than ten minutes.

The umpires should stop time for enforced stoppages such as accidents and penalty strokes, and restart it when whistling or signalling for play to resume. Players and umpires should endeavour to keep the length of such stoppages to a minimum.

Choice of ends

It is customary for the captains of the two teams to meet with the umpires and for the home captain to toss a coin, giving the visitor the call. The captain winning the toss may choose either which end to attack in the first half, or to have possession of the ball at the start of the game. The winner having made his choice, the opposing team automatically has the second option.

The umpires should not normally indicate which ends they will take until the team captains have made their own decisions. Umpires are advised to note which team has possession to start the game so as to avoid confusion at the beginning of the second half.

Starting and restarting the game

The pass-back

The game is started, and restarted after half-time and after each goal, by a pass-back from the centre of the pitch. The pass-back at the beginning of the game is taken by the team which did not make a choice of ends, and by the opposing team after half-time; after a goal the game is restarted by the team against whom the goal was scored.

For the pass-back the ball is placed in the centre of the pitch and all players, other than the striker, take up their positions in their own half of the field. No member of the team without possession may be within 5 yds of the ball.

The pass-back may be hit or pushed, and must be directed along the halfway line or into the defending half of the field. Having taken the pass-back, the striker must not play the ball again nor approach within playing distance, until it has been touched by another player of either team. Time wasting is not allowed.

The bully

A bully is taken to restart the game after certain stoppages, e.g. an accident not caused by a foul, the ball lodging in a goalkeeper's pad or in the clothing of another player or an umpire, or any unforeseen incident that warrants the game being stopped, e.g. the ball splitting.

The bully is taken on a spot chosen by the umpire in whose half the incident occurred. No bully may take place inside the 16-yard area.

To take the bully, a player from each team stands squarely facing the side line, left shoulder towards the goal he is attacking, with the ball on the ground between them. Each player taps the ground behind the ball, and then, with the flat face of the stick, taps the opponent's stick above the ball, three times alternately before attempting to play the ball. The bully is completed and the ball in play when it has been touched by one of the players taking the bully.

Until the bully is completed, all other players must be at least 5 yds from the ball.

Ball in and out of play

A ball is in play until it has passed wholly over the side lines or back lines even though the player playing the ball may be outside the playing area.

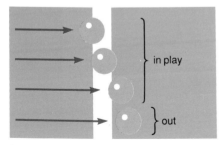

The ball is not out of play if it rebounds off the umpire (standing on the field of play) or off the goal post, cross-bar or corner flag, into the field of play.

The push-in/hit-in

When the whole of the ball passes over either side line it is pushed or hit in, in any direction from the point where it crossed the line.

The rules state that:

● the push-in/hit-in must be taken by an opponent of the player who last touched the ball before it crossed over the side line
● the ball must be pushed or hit. It must not be lifted deliberately nor rise dangerously. The striker must move the ball – just to touch it with the stick is not sufficient
● the ball must be placed on the line at the point where it crossed the line
● no player of the opposing team shall be within 5 yds of the ball
● the striker shall not play the ball again, nor remain or approach within playing distance of the ball, until it has

been touched by another player of either team. The player taking the push-in or hit-in may stand in the field of play.

If the umpire considers that a player is deliberately standing nearer than 5 yds to delay the push-in or hit-in, he need not stop the game.

Penalties for infringements

For any breach of the rules a free hit is awarded to the opposing team.

If the umpire considers that a defender has deliberately breached the rules inside the 25-yard area but outside the circle, a penalty corner should be awarded against the defending side.

The 16-yard hit-out

When the ball is sent out of play over the back line by a player of the attacking team and no goal is scored, or if the ball is sent over the back line by one of the defending team from a distance of 25 yds or more, play is resumed by a hit or push taken by one of the defending team exactly opposite the place where the ball crossed the back line, not more

▲ *Ball correctly positioned for a push-in or hit-in from the side line*

than 16 yds from the inner edge of that line.

The ball must be stationary before it is hit or pushed. It must not be raised intentionally. It must be moved from its original position; just touching it with the stick is not deemed to be a hit.

The opposing team must be at least 5 yds from the ball. Having taken the hit-out, the striker must not play the ball again nor remain nor approach within playing distance until it has been touched by another player of either team.

Push or hit from back line

A push or hit from the back line is awarded to the attacking team when the whole of the ball, having last been touched by one of the defending team within the 25-yard area, passes unintentionally out of play behind the back line.

The following are regulations concerning a push or hit from the back line:

● the hit or push is taken by one of the attacking team. In doing so, the striker must move the ball from its original position

- the ball must be motionless on the back line within 5 yds of the corner flag
- all players of the defending team must be at least 5 yds from the ball
- should the striker raise the ball deliberately or dangerously, approach it or play it again before anyone else has touched it, a free hit is awarded to the defence
- while the ball need not be stopped before a shot at goal is made, any shot which is in itself dangerous or could lead to dangerous play will be penalised.

Note (1) In order to make the best use of a hit-out, it should be taken without delay, but with regard for the 5 yds rule. (2) If an attacking hit from the corner area enters the circle in the air it will almost certainly either be dangerous in itself or cause danger, and should be penalised immediately.

Scoring a goal

The scoring of goals is the object of the game – the team scoring the most goals is the winner of the match. If no goals or an equal number of goals are scored, the game is a draw.

The following are regulations concerning the scoring of a goal:

- the whole of the ball must pass over the goal line between the posts and under the cross-bar
- the ball must have been hit by, or glanced off, the stick of an attacking player in the circle. If, after having been hit by an attacker in the circle, the ball comes into contact with the person or stick of a defender and then enters the goal, a goal is scored
- should the goal post and/or the cross-bar collapse, the umpire must judge whether the ball crossed the line where the goal would have been, and give the appropriate award.

Fouls

Fouls are largely the result of faulty stickwork, footwork, or positioning of the body. Refer to page 20 for the relevant penalties. Fouls may be divided into eight categories, as follows.

Dangerous play

- A ball above the height of the shoulder must not be played with any part of the stick. Exceptionally, the goalkeeper in the circle may stop (though not propel) the ball above the shoulder with the stick, but only if it is safe to do so. No player's stick should be raised so that it endangers, intimidates or hampers another player when playing, approaching or stopping the ball.
- A player must not hit the ball in such a way that it rises dangerously or may lead to dangerous play. A scoop which raises the ball in a controlled manner is permissible; however, any pass made into the circle must not be raised deliberately. Elsewhere on the pitch a lifted ball which is dangerous, either in flight

▲ *No player's stick should be raised so that it endangers, intimidates or hampers another player when playing, approaching or stopping the ball*

or on landing, will be penalised.

However, opponents who approach within 5 yds of a player receiving a high ball will be considered to be creating a dangerous situation and penalised accordingly.

It is totally prohibited to lift the ball from the ground and hit it again while it is still in the air.

● A player who hits wildly into an opponent will be penalised for dangerous play.

Backsticks

A player must not hit the ball with the rounded side of the stick. This is a common fault with beginners when attempting to hit the ball on their left side. If the ball merely hits the back of the stick and no advantage results, no offence has taken place.

Interference

A player must not strike, hit, hook, hold or interfere with another player's stick. For example, an attacker's stick may not be held down by a defender's stick.

Handling the ball

The ball may be moved with the stick only; a player must not stop the ball with his hand either on the ground or in the air, nor may he catch it. (But *see* page 17 on a goalkeeper's privileges.)

A player who uses his hand to protect himself from a dangerously raised ball will not be penalised.

Kicking the ball

A player may not deliberately use a foot to stop or propel the ball, but it is not necessarily a foul if the ball strikes the foot and the player concerned gains no advantage. Neither may the foot be used to support the stick in resisting a tackle, though it can be used to support the stick when stopping the ball.

Handling opponents

A player must not trip, shove, push, charge, strike at, or in any way personally handle another player. For example, a defender commits a foul if, by putting his stick just in front of an attacker, he so trips that player.

Pushing

If an attacker who has overrun the ball is pushed by a defender close behind, the defender has committed a foul by handling the attacker. It is immaterial whether the attacker would have recovered the ball.

Charging

If a defender attempts to force an attacker away from the ball by charging him with his shoulder or elbowing him off course, the defender commits a foul.

Obstruction

A player must not obstruct by running between an opponent and the ball, if that opponent is within playing distance and trying to play the ball, nor may he interpose any part of the body or stick between an opponent and the ball such that the opponent is denied a fair chance of playing the ball. A player who receives the ball when being closely marked from behind should move away quickly with the ball so as not to interfere with the potential tackler.

Interference without stick

A player can only play the game with his own stick (or one legally substituted for it) in his hand. For example, a goalkeeper who continues to defend without holding his stick is fouling.

Goalkeeper's privileges

While the ball is in the circle the goalkeeper may kick the ball and stop it with any part of the body including the hand. The goalkeeper is also allowed latitude with balls which rebound from the body or hand, but he is not allowed to strike at or propel the ball with any part of the body except the feet and legs, nor is he permitted to throw the ball. The hand may be used, however, to deflect the ball over the cross-bar or round the goal posts.

Protective equipment may be worn – in fact, wearing it should be encouraged – but this does not give latitude for misbehaviour towards other players that would not be safe without such protection. Such misbehaviour should be penalised. A full head helmet should always be worn, preferably with additional neck/throat protection.

The goalkeeper should not be permitted to make unnecessary changes of clothing for penalty strokes, but he is permitted to remove headgear and/or gloves. If the goalkeeper is substituted, time may need to be allowed for the substitute to put on protective equipment.

Offside

As in many field games where scoring is by means of goals, some restrictions are applied to prevent players gaining an advantage by lingering near the opponent's goal ready to score from short range. This restriction is known as the offside rule: some players find it difficult to understand.

As the infringement of this rule causes an immediate breakdown of the attack and gives a free hit to the defending team, it is necessary that all its details should be clearly understood.

The rule requires that, at the moment that the ball is played by an attacker, any other attacker inside the 25-yard area must either be behind the ball (which usually applies when the defence has been beaten) or that there be at least two defenders between their own goal and that attacker. Note that the two defenders need not necessarily include the goalkeeper.

The attackers should be penalised only if the attacker(s) in or having been in an offside position actually gained an advantage.

The important factor is the player's position when the ball is played, not when it is received by that or another attacker.

The penalty for offside is a free hit awarded to the defending team.

Examples

(1) In fig. 4 (page 18) the Left Wing is offside because, when the ball was last played, there was only one defender between that player and the back line.

The umpire is slightly nearer the back line than the second defender.

(2) In fig. 5 (page 18) the Inside Left is offside in the circle because, when the ball was hit, there was only one defender – the goalkeeper – between the

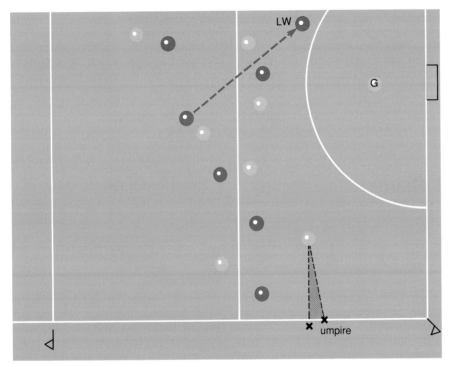

▲ Fig. 4 *Left Wing offside*

player and the back line. Being level with the second defender – i.e. so that there are not two defenders actually *between* an attacker and the back line – is offside.

The umpire has closed in, in order to see more clearly in the congested circle, and is still level with, or slightly ahead of, the second defender.

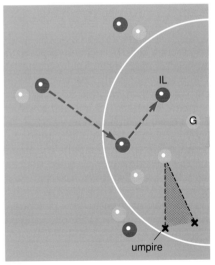

▲ Fig. 5 *Inside Left offside*

(3) In fig. 6 the Right Wing is in the opposing 25-yard area and, with only one defender in that area, is therefore in an offside position.

The umpire is at the 25-yard line to see whether the other forwards cross the line before another attacker hits the ball, making them offside.

(4) In fig. 7 the Inside Left is offside because the defenders have been left behind and, when the ball was hit, there was only the goalkeeper between that player and the back line.

The umpire is slightly ahead of the second defender.

(5) In fig. 8 the Inside Left shoots at goal and follows up. The goalkeeper clears the ball back to the same player, who shoots again. Meanwhile, another attacker – the Inside Right – having rushed forwards at the first shot in anticipation of a rebound, is left offside by failing to move back before the second shot is made.

The umpire has closed in, and should be level with the ball.

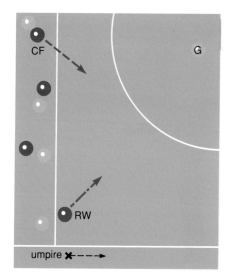

▲ Fig. 6 Right Wing offside

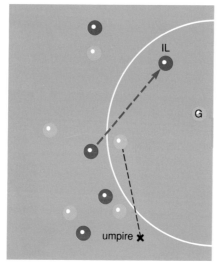

▲ Fig. 7 Inside Left offside

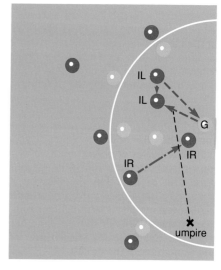

▲ Fig. 8 Inside Right offside

19

Penalties

Penalties can be grouped under three headings.

- Penalty stroke for serious defensive breaches in the circle.
- Penalty corner for deliberate defensive breaches in the 25-yard area outside the circle, and most other breaches in the circle.
- Free hits for all fouls other than defensive fouls in the circle and deliberate infringements in the defending 25-yard area.

In addition to the above penalties, the umpire has the power to warn or suspend any player or players guilty of serious misconduct or rough or dangerous play. This may be done by showing a coloured disciplinary card: green indicates a warning; yellow indicates a temporary suspension for not less than five minutes; red indicates suspension for the remainder of the match.

▲ *Umpire showing a player a green disciplinary card – a warning*

Penalty stroke

A penalty stroke is awarded for:

● an accidental defensive foul that denies an otherwise probable goal
● persistent defensive breaking of the back line at a penalty corner
● deliberate breaches to deny possession or likely possession of the ball to the attack of the free hit rule, the rule governing putting the ball back into play within the circle, and that governing what players may or may not do.

A penalty stroke is *not* awarded for a deliberate defensive foul against an attacker who does not have and is unlikely to gain possession of the ball, no matter how bad the foul is.

Procedure

The penalty stroke is taken by a player nominated by the attacking team from a spot 7 yds in front of the centre of the goal line. The ball may be flicked, scooped or pushed at any height. The striker may take one step forwards, though his back foot must not pass the front foot before the ball is moved. The striker is not allowed to follow up the shot.

The stroke is defended by the goalkeeper on the pitch at the time, unless he is incapacitated or suspended, in which case a substitute is nominated, who may put on protective equipment. The goalkeeper must stand with both feet on the goal line, and after the umpire has blown the whistle he must not move either foot before the ball is played. The usual goalkeeper's privileges are retained.

All other players must be beyond the 25-yard line and should stand towards the sides of the pitch, not in the goalkeeper's line of vision.

The umpire in control of the stroke must be able to see both players and the goal. An advantageous position is slightly behind and to the right of the striker. It is general practice for the other umpire to stand on the back line to check whether the ball has crossed the goal line, e.g. to watch for the goalkeeper catching the ball with a hand behind the goal line.

Completion

A goal is scored if the ball crosses the goal line; a penalty goal is awarded if a foul by the goalkeeper prevents the ball entering the goal.

The stroke is completed and the game restarted by a 16-yard hit in front of the centre of the goal if the ball passes out of the circle or comes to rest in the circle. A ball caught by the goalkeeper or lodged in his pads is considered to be 'at rest'.

If the attacker fouls, the stroke is over and the game restarts with a 16-yard hit. Taking the stroke before the whistle is blown, feinting at striking the ball or any deliberate action which induces the goalkeeper to move either or both feet are regarded as fouls.

Penalty corner

A penalty corner is awarded for:

● accidental breaches in the circle which do not prevent probable goals
● deliberate defensive breaches in the circle not involving the ball
● accidental breaches of the rules governing free hits and restarting play from hits within the circle

▲ *The 'injector' of the penalty corner must have at least one foot behind the back line, off the pitch – the method shown here is therefore not permitted*

- deliberate defensive breaches outside the circle but within the 25-yard area.

These breaches are of the rules governing what players may or may not do, free hits and hits for putting the ball back into play.

The rules concerning a penalty corner are as follows:

- the hit or push is taken on whichever side the attack chooses, at a point not less than 10 yds from the nearer goal post
- the ball must be on the back line and be hit or pushed by an attacker (the 'injector') who must have at least one foot behind the back line, off the pitch. The ball must not be lifted deliberately nor rise dangerously
- apart from the injector, all members of the attacking team must be on the field of play, at least 5 yds from the ball, and must have their feet and sticks outside the circle
- not more than five of the defending team – it may be any five – must stand (with both feet and sticks) behind their back line or goal line, and at least 5 yds from the ball. The remainder of the team

▲ *Not more than five of the defending team must stand behind their back line or goal line, and at least 5 yds from the ball, at a penalty corner*

must stand beyond the centre line

● if players from either team move into the circle before the ball is hit, the umpire may require the hit to be re-taken

● if the striker approaches or plays the ball again before anyone has touched it, a free hit is awarded to the defence

● unless the ball has been touched by a defender's stick or body, no shot at goal may be made unless one of the attackers, not necessarily the one who takes the shot, first stops the ball dead on the ground, or the ball first comes to a stop on the ground, outside the circle. There is no requirement that the ball be stopped again before the actual shot is made

● the first *hit* at goal must not cross the goal line above the height of the side-boards and back-board (18 in) unless it has touched the stick or person of a defender. Scoop and flick shots at any height are allowed, provided that they cause no danger

● no goal can be scored directly by the player taking the penalty corner

● if the ball travels more than 5 yds beyond the outer edge of the circle or is touched by the stick or body of a defen-der, the penalty corner is deemed to be over and the ball in normal play. Although there is then no requirement for the ball to be stopped, any stroke or shot is subject to the dangerous play rule (*see* page 14).

Free hit

● All players of the opposing team must be at least 5 yds from the ball. However, for a free hit to the attacking team within 5 yds of the circle, players of both teams, apart from the striker, must be 5 yds from the ball.

● The ball must be stationary and must be hit or pushed. A scoop or flick is not allowed. A free hit must not be lifted deliberately, nor must the ball rise dangerously.

● The player taking the hit must not play the ball again nor approach or remain within playing distance of the ball until it has been played or touched by another player's stick.

● If the player hits at but misses the ball, the stroke may be taken again.

● The ball must be moved; it is not sufficient for the striker to tap the top of it before a team mate takes over.

● For infringements by the player taking the hit, a free hit is awarded to the other side.

The free hit is taken on the spot where the infringement occurred. However, if a free hit is awarded to the defending team within the 16-yard area it may be taken from any spot within this area on a line drawn parallel to the side line from where the foul occurred; and if the breach of the rule occurred within the circle the free hit may be taken any-where within the circle if the player so wishes.

A player who gains extra advantage by taking the free hit in the wrong place should be penalised, but the umpire should try to avoid the problem before the hit is taken.

Control of the game

Umpires

Two umpires are responsible for the control of the game. They must know all the rules of the game thoroughly, and should be capable of applying them. Quite often a decision rests on the umpire's opinion. Was the ball sent over the back line intentionally or not? Is a player in an offside position interfering with the game? Is a particular stroke dangerous?

Each umpire controls half the field (the division being the centre line) for the whole game without changing ends. When standing on the side line facing into the field, the umpire is primarily responsible for decisions on the half of the field on the right. It is customary that there is an imaginary diagonal from one 25-yard line to the other, and in this quarter each umpire deals with fouls coming towards him from the other circle. The division of responsibility *must* be agreed by the umpires before the game. Each umpire gives decisions on the hit-in down the whole length of his side line and on the fouls in the 5-yard area. Each umpire is *wholly* responsible for decisions on back line hits, penalty corners, penalty strokes, goals and free hits in *his* respective circle.

An umpire's duties are as follows.

● To ensure fair and safe play, subject to the advantage rule – i.e. the umpire should refrain from penalising in cases where he is satisfied that by doing so he would be giving an advantage to the offending team.

For example, an attacking player, although being obstructed near the circle, may still be able to press home the attack and make a shot at goal; should the umpire penalise the obstruction and award a free hit, the defenders would be able to recover and mark their opponents closely.

● To stop the game for an infringement, awarding the appropriate penalty indicated by an arm signal. In the case of misconduct or rough or dangerous play, the umpire has the power to warn or suspend the offending player as well as penalising him. The umpire may also stop play if an accident or any unforeseen incident makes this necessary.

● To whistle to indicate the resumption of play after time has been stopped.

● To keep time, unless there is a separate timekeeper. The umpires should agree who should start and stop each half. It is normal for the umpire in whose half the ball is *not* to end each half. It is essential that both umpires check the time: an exchange of signals at two minutes before the end of each half is usual. Time for all stoppages, including penalty strokes, is stopped and restarted when the whistle is blown for play to resume. The umpire who suspends a player controls the time of that suspension.

● To keep a written record of the goals scored.

Umpire's position

● Each umpire controls the same half of the field for the whole game; the goal is to the right when facing into the pitch. The umpire is also responsible for dealing with fouls in the area divided by the blue line in fig. 9.

● The offside rule is a question of alignment of players, which can only be judged correctly by viewing the play at right angles to the side line. As play comes into the 25-yard area the umpire should be slightly nearer the back line than the second defender or the foremost attacking player. Thus any attacker on the right is in an offside position.

● The umpire should normally keep outside the field of play between the centre line and the 25-yard line, moving up and down to ensure a clear view of play. From about the 25-yard line, movement should curve towards the nearer goal post so as to be able to see clearly incidents in the circle, but also so as to follow play inwards from the wing without losing sight of players behind. Rather than be forced over the back line, and thus risk losing sight of the line between the goal posts, umpires

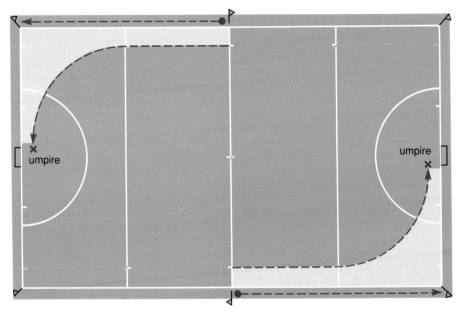

▲ *Fig. 9 Umpires' positions: the red areas show the approximate range of movement; the blue lines, the division of responsibility*

must be ready to move quickly backwards if play moves towards the back line or nearer side line, both to avoid impeding players and to keep all players within the angle of vision. The umpire's path resembles the shape of a hockey stick.

The umpire must be able to see the ball at all times.

Timekeepers

It is permissible to have timekeepers. It is recommended that two timekeepers be appointed and that they stay on the same side of the pitch as that where the team substitutes are, opposite the centre line.

Timekeepers' duties are:

● to take the time when the umpire starts each half
● to stop and restart time for stoppages as indicated by the umpires
● to sound a whistle or hooter for half-time and full-time.

Technical tables

At most international and major tournaments and matches, technical tables are used. The judges at the technical table keep a complete record of the match; the report sheet shows the names of the squads and umpires, and may indicate any substitutions which are made. The goal scorers' names are recorded with the time and whether the goal was the outcome of a penalty corner or penalty stroke, or from open play.

The judges are responsible for timekeeping; they take the time from the umpire's whistle at the start, sound their hooter for stopping each half, and stop and start the clock for stoppages as indicated by the umpires.

The table controls all substitutions and may record the time when the substitutions take place. Disciplinary cards and the time at which they are awarded are also recorded.

Understanding the game

To the casual observer, hockey can sometimes appear complex. In fact, it is an exceedingly simple game once the basic concepts, skills and rules have been learnt and understood.

Phases of the game

There are two distinct phases in a game of hockey:

● the attacking phase – when one's own team has the ball, and
● the defending phase – when the opposition has the ball.

The objectives, for both the individual and the team, for each phase are as follows.

Attacking phase
● To keep possession.
● To move the ball forwards and penetrate the opposing defence at the earliest opportunity.

- To create shooting and goal-scoring opportunities in the opposing circle.
- To score goals.

Defending phase
- To regain possession at the earliest opportunity.
- To prevent the ball being played or carried forwards, i.e. to prevent the opposition penetrating one's own defence.
- To deny the opposition shooting and goal-scoring opportunities in one's own circle.
- To avoid conceding goals.

The following skills are required to achieve the objectives in each phase.

Attacking phase
- Control of and composure on the ball.
- Ability to run with the ball.
- Ability to dribble and dodge.
- Ability to pass.
- Ability to receive a pass.
- Ability to create and convert goal-scoring opportunities.

Defending phase
- Ability to mark.
- Ability to delay, channel and close down opponents.
- Ability to intercept and tackle.
- Ability to prevent and deny shooting/goal-scoring opportunities.
- Ability to protect and defend the goal – effective goalkeeping.

The styles of play demanded during each of these phases can be described as follows.

- Attacking phase – fluid, expansive and creative.
- Defending phase – disciplined, organised and secure.

In similar fashion, the game's principles of play are determined by these two phases.

- In attack – possession, speed, support, penetration, concentration, width and mobility.
- In defence – depth, delay, balance, concentration, organisation, security and speed.

To perform effectively in the game, players must have a full understanding of the objectives, styles and principles of play required of them during the different phases of the game and in the different areas of the pitch. Most importantly, effective team play is dependent on individual players mastering and performing the basic techniques and skills.

Zonal priorities

Fig. 10 depicts the zonal priorities on the field.

- Attacking zone – speed, penetration and creativity.
- Build-up/consolidation zone – possession, control, deception and construction.
- Defending zone – discipline, safety and organisation.

There are three basic factors which underpin the skills of the game.

- Grip.
- Footwork.
- Vision.

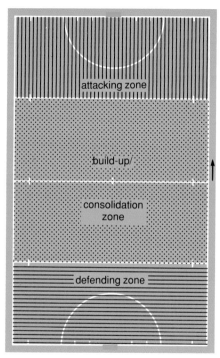

Fig. 10 Zonal priorities

Grip

Mastery of the grip is an important element in the acquisition and execution of all skills. Methods of employing the correct grip should be introduced early in the development process.

The left hand holds the top of the stick so that a 'V' is formed by the thumb and forefinger down the back of the stick. This grip will result in the flat (hitting) face of the stick facing the ground. The right hand should be placed a third to halfway down the shaft of the stick. The rotational movement of the stick from open to reverse stick and back is controlled by the left hand, while the right hand provides added support and control as the stick is rotated through it. Some players prefer to extend the index finger of the right hand down the shaft of the stick to further aid control. Both hands must feel comfortable when the stick is held in the open and reverse stick position.

Fig. 11 Gripping the stick

Footwork

Players must learn to move forwards, sideways and backwards while maintaining close contact of the ball. Good footwork will increase a player's mobility and is essential in creating space and time when under pressure.

Vision

When in control of the ball, a player must be able to see as much as possible of what is occurring over the rest of the pitch. The position in which the ball is controlled and carried in relation to the body will assist or restrict vision. If the ball is held in front of and slightly to the right of the body with the upper body inclined forwards, the player will have good vision of what is happening around him. If the ball is kept too close to the feet, the player's body will inevitably be bent over the ball and his vision reduced accordingly.

It is essential to ensure that in developing close control, vision and awareness are not impaired or restricted.

▲ *In developing close control, vision must not be impaired*

Attacking play

Controlling the ball

Control and composure are essential when players are attempting to retain possession of the ball in the game, especially when being pressured and harassed by opponents intent on dispossessing them.

Practices which allow players to keep, manipulate, juggle and manoeuvre the ball with the stick will develop control, confidence and composure on the ball.

Running with the ball

Running with the ball encompasses a number of techniques and requires the player to 'carry' or propel the ball with the stick, but without any exaggerated or complex movement of stick and ball. This should permit them to look up and assess the situation before choosing the next move.

Running with the ball is most effective when there is plenty of time and space to operate and where there are no opponents in close proximity; it can be used also to run past and beat an opponent if necessary.

Technique

● Hold the body as near upright as possible, holding the stick at the top with the left hand.

● The stick and ball should be kept well out in front of the body and slightly to the right, so making it easier to run at speed and to look up while doing so.

● Good balanced footwork is essential, as is the ability to 'scan' ahead to read the pattern of play. Players must learn to recognise when they should pass and when they should run with the ball. Both skills require close control.

Dribbling

The (Indian) dribble forms the basis of all stickwork. Once mastered, it allows a player to move to the more complex skills of feinting, dodging, 'dummying' and eliminating opponents.

▲ *Running with the ball*

▲ *Competition for possession*

Technique

● When employing this skill, the ball is tapped and dragged from left to right with a rolling action of the hands and wrists.

● It is the left hand that controls the twisting, rotational movement of the stick while the right hand generates the pulling and pushing action necessary for moving the ball. The right hand also provides the control and stability for action.

● Young players should first learn to move the ball from open to reverse stick and back again while stationary. Once this has been mastered, the skill can be attempted at walking, then jogging and eventually running speed.

Dodging

Dodging is performed by combining and co-ordinating the movements of body, stick and ball. The object at all times is to give the impression that you are moving in a certain direction, then suddenly, when the opponent is committed to covering the first move, you change direction and move past the opponent on the other side.

Although some considerable time should be devoted to acquiring the techniques and skills required for beating an opponent in one-to-one situations, it must be stressed that still the best way to beat an opponent is to pass the ball around or past him.

Passing

Passing is often described as the building block of team play. Many coaches agree – if you can't pass, you can't play.

A pass involves two players – the passer and the receiver – but includes a number of elements which influence and affect the outcome of the pass. The most important element is the harmony between passer and receiver. It is therefore imperative for players to learn to pass and receive the ball early in their playing careers so that they can recognise and exploit the options open to them in the game.

Effective passing depends on a number of simple but nevertheless fundamental team principles.

● The player must be **A**ware of the positioning of team mates and opponents.

● The player must be **B**alanced.
● The player must have **C**ontrol of the ball.

This is the **ABC** of passing: together with knowing **when** to pass and **when** to hold the ball, this adds up to 'reading' the game.

There are six main types of pass used in the modern game.

Hit

Used for passing the ball quickly over long distances, for shooting at goal, and when taking free hits or hits-in from the side and back line.

Push

The most commonly used pass in the game. While it lacks the speed of the hit, it is more effective in terms of accuracy.

Reverse push

Most effective when passing from left to right over short distances, and when no open stick pass is possible. Usually played square or behind square.

Slap

Very similar to the push, and used almost as often. But while the push is most effective over short distances, the slap can be used to make long, powerful, penetrative passes.

Flick

An extension of the push. Used to lift the ball into the air, either as a long overhead pass, or a short pass, or a shot at goal over an opponent's stick or a prone goalkeeper.

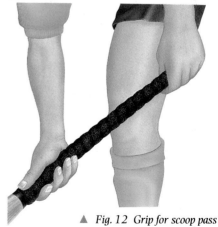

▲ *Fig. 12 Grip for scoop pass*

33

▲ *The hit*

Scoop

An alternative aerial pass in which the right foot and shoulder are brought forwards to achieve the shovelling action needed to lift the ball high over an opponent or several opponents. This requires an adjustment to the grip and body position.

Receiving the ball

In any team game which involves passing, it is essential for players to be able to receive and gain instant control of the ball. The first touch on the ball is crucial when receiving. If instant control is achieved by the receiver, he will create extra space and time in which to prepare for the next move.

When receiving the ball, the open or reverse stick will be used, depending on where the ball is received and what action the player has to take next.

There are occasions when the player receiving the ball will need to stop it dead. Generally speaking, the receiver of a pass will be required to bring the ball under control and re-position it in preparation for the next move whether it be a pass, a dribble or a shot. Players must learn to perform this skill in minimum time.

The ball can be received while the player is stationary or on the move.

Shooting and goal-scoring

All players enjoy scoring spectacular goals. In reality, all goals are good goals, no matter how simple they may appear.

Good strikers not only know **how** to shoot, but also **when** and **where** to shoot. Although it is true that the more strikes one has on goal the more one is likely to score, a good striker knows when to shoot and when to pass to a team mate in a more favourable position.

All shots on goal should be on target. Saved shots often provide rebounds which in turn can lead to secondary strike opportunities. Coaches should encourage players to follow up shots on goal.

Many goal-scoring opportunities appear suddenly and awkwardly. High levels of concentration and sound technical ability are required to take advantage of these half-chances when they arise.

Good strikers must be prepared to chase lost causes, get on the end of crosses, pick up deflections and collect passes that arrive at different heights and angles, plus control the ball and make a shot at goal, often under pressure from defenders, and in the minimum time and space available.

The key to becoming a top goal-scorer lies in possessing the desire, determination, courage and commitment to succeed.

Defending play

The team in possession of the ball aims to retain possession for long enough to launch an attack and score a goal. The primary aim of the defending team is to prevent the attackers from doing so, and to regain possession of the ball in order to initiate its own attack on the opposite goal.

Generally, possession is regained by intercepting badly timed and misdirected passes, or by tackling an opponent who is still in possession of the ball.

Intercepting

In order to intercept the ball, defenders must mark tightly, read the game and anticipate the actions of the opponents. Interceptions do away with the need to tackle, and often result in clean, high quality possession from which to launch rapid and effective counter-attacks.

If an interception attempt fails, the defender must re-position himself in order to channel, shadow and close down the attacker with the aim of dispossessing him with a tackle.

Tackling

While the ultimate aim of making a tackle is to regain possession, sometimes it may be necessary to employ a tackle with the purpose of putting the ball out of play, thereby buying time for the tackler's team to reorganise defensively.

While it is unusual for players to employ more than one or two types of tackle in a game, it is important for all players to be able to execute all three main types of tackle.

Jab

The advantage of this tackle is that it can be executed with speed and surprise. It is sometimes used as a decoy to set up a secondary tackle or to force an error out of the attacker, thus slowing down the attack or putting the ball out of play.

The stick is held in the left hand and is lunged at the ball like the head of a striking snake. The right hand is used occasionally to provide support in the preparatory stage.

The left leg leads, as in fencing, providing balance and control for the movement and power of the recovery if the first tackle is unsuccessful.

Open stick

This is probably the most commonly used tackle in the game. It can be performed while standing still or on the move. It is also possible to make this tackle close to or well away from the feet.

The left foot once again leads the movement. The right foot provides the pivotal support required to change direction if the first attempt fails.

If performed when standing still, the stick is nearly always used as a barrier – the block tackle. When performed on the move, a more upright stick is used, but it is stationary. It is important for defenders to position themselves goalside and to the right of the attacker before attempting the tackle.

Reverse stick

The game's rules forbid contact with an opponent's body or stick when making a tackle. Therefore, it is essential for the

▲ *Block tackle*

defender to get into a position which allows the tackle to be made level with or in front of his own body.

Although occasionally it may be possible to use two hands when employing the reverse stick tackle, the position of the defender and the way in which the ball is normally carried by attackers (i.e. in front of and to the right of their bodies) makes it necessary to tackle one-handed. The further away from the defender that the tackle is made, the flatter the stick must be to the ground. Tackles made with flat sticks are more effective when playing on artificial surfaces or indoors.

The main points to remember when tackling are:

● watch the ball, not the stick or the body of the player in possession
● time the tackle correctly; don't be tempted to dive in
● recognise when to tackle and which tackle to use
● channel the attacking player on to his reverse stick side (the defender's open stick side).

▲ *Close man-to-man marking*

All these points demand balanced footwork and sharp reflexes.

Marking

Marking forms the basis for all defensive play. The primary aims of marking are to discourage passes to a particular player or, if a pass is made, to intercept it or harass or distract the player to enforce an error, or to tackle the player if he receives possession of the ball.

There are three main methods of organising a team's defence:

- man-to-man marking (one-to-one)
- zonal marking
- a combination of both.

Man-to-man marking

The basic concept in this system is when the opposition have the ball, each player from the defending team marks an assigned opponent. Each defending player must:

- stay as close as possible to his opponent
- make it as difficult as possible for his opponent to receive a pass

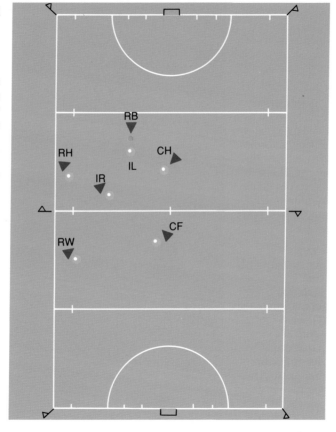

Key
player with ball
other attacker
defender

◀ Fig. 13
Man-to-man marking
system

- retain a position between his opponents and the goal
- adopt a position in which he can see the opponent and the ball.

Zonal marking

As the name suggests, in this system defending players form a zone as soon as possession is lost. Each defender takes responsibility for any opponent who comes into his zone of defence. The zone concentrates and tightens marking in the area of greatest danger. Discipline and the retention of organisation are critical to the system's success.

Combination marking systems

The most effective marking systems are those which utilise a combination of zonal and man-to-man systems.

This style relies on tight man-to-man marking of all opposition players immediately around the ball, with the cover defence employing zonal marking.

The crucial moment for the team is when possession is lost. Failure to react quickly can allow the opposition to gain numerical superiority in the danger area, penetrating the defence's circle.

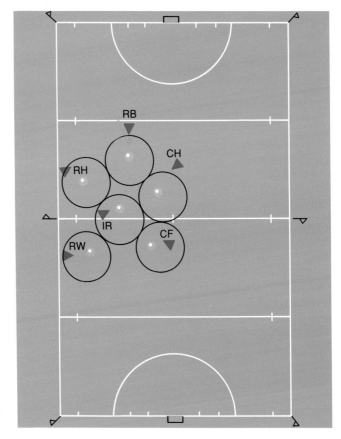

◀ Fig. 14 Zonal marking system

40

Goalkeeping

The goalkeeper's role in the team is to protect the goal.

All goalkeeping actions should start from the accepted position of balanced readiness. This position can be used as a springboard for any save or move that is required.

Low shots directed straight at the goalkeeper should be stopped with the pads. Then the ball should be pushed or kicked towards the side lines, for safety, never back to the middle of the circle.

There are occasions when the goalkeeper will be required to make saves using the stick or the hand. Usually the ball will be in the air, in which case the hand should be used. If, however, the ball is placed beyond the reach of the goalkeeper's hands, the stick can be used. As with the use of the pads, the hand is used to cushion and control the shot. The ball must not be held. As the ball falls to the ground, it must be cleared in a controlled fashion using the stick or the pads.

In developing these skills, goalkeepers and their coaches must continue to give attention to good, balanced footwork. It is this that sets the goalkeeper in a position from which to make the save.

All good goalkeepers must know how to command the circle, both physically and vocally. They should not be afraid of marshalling the defence, and they should always look to be not only the last line of defence, but also the launching pad of many attacks.

Equipment

Great advances have been made in recent years in the field of goalkeeping equipment. Today's game requires the goalkeeper to wear a large range of protective equipment. Here is a checklist:

- ice hockey style helmet and strong visor
- throat protector
- chest pad
- shoulder and elbow pads
- gloves
- abdominal protector
- genital protector (or 'box')
- padded shorts and thigh protectors
- lightweight leg guards
- knee pads
- lightweight kickers
- boots or other suitable footwear.

▲ *Goalkeeper's position of balanced readiness*

41

Helmet,
visor
and
throat
protector

Chest pad

Padded shorts

Gloves

Leg guards

Kickers

42

Restarts and set pieces

Every game contains a large number of stoppages. Restarts and set pieces are an essential and integral part of the game and, as such, should be understood, rehearsed and perfected in order to derive maximum advantage from them.

The most common situations from which restarts and set pieces are made are:

- free hits
- hits-in from the side line
- hits-in from the back line
- penalty corners.

(Other restarts such as the push-back and the bully have been referred to earlier.)

Free hits

In order to derive the most advantage from a free hit, the team in possession should attempt to take it as quickly as possible and certainly before the defending team has had time to reorganise.

If the opportunity for taking an effective free hit is not there, the team in possession must fall back on well drilled routines.

The objectives for each free hit should be known to all players in the team. They are:

- do not speculate, **calculate** (particularly in the defending zone)
- wherever possible, move the ball forwards near or into the danger areas in and around the opposition circle
- the player on the ball must decide what happens, but it is the players off the ball who, by moving into or creating space, dictate what happens next
- keep possession.

Hits-in from the side line

The same principles and objectives of the free hit apply to the hit-in from the side line.

Hits-in from the back line

Opportunities to take hits-in from the back line quickly are rare because the defending team almost inevitably has time to reorganise itself.

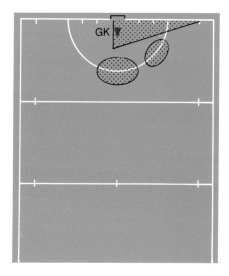

▲ *Fig. 15 Hit-in from the back line: danger areas*

The attacking players should manoeuvre to receive and control the ball on the open stick side, and in a position that allows them to attack their markers on their reverse stick side.

For the defenders, the problems are different, if not exactly the opposite. Defending players will be expected to counter every move by the attacking side and prevent the ball being received by the attackers in the danger areas. The goalkeeper is the key defender: the team defence should always allow the goalkeeper to have a clear view of the ball.

Occasionally, attacking teams will try to move a well organised defence by playing the ball short and then working it into the danger areas. Defending sides should be alert to this and allocate the task of closing down the player with the ball to specific defenders.

Penalty corners

The penalty corner is a unique aspect of the game in the sense that the rules place restrictions on both the attacking and the defending sides. These restrictions must be taken into consideration when executing attacking moves or when defending against them.

Attacking

Attacking at penalty corners is a matter of good team work, involving individual skill and collective effort. In preparing for a penalty corner, it is vital to consider the following available options.

● To have a direct shot on goal.
● If this is not possible, it may be necessary to move the ball into another area of the circle from which a shot may be made.

The attacking team always has the advantage at penalty corners because the defending team can only try to anticipate what is going to happen.

To retain this advantage, the attacking team should have at its disposal a series of set piece variations to employ

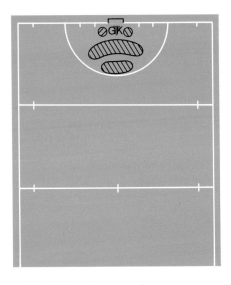

▲ *Fig. 16 Penalty corner: danger areas*

according to the situation. The more simple and direct these variations are, the more likely they are to succeed.

Defending

Only four players and the goalkeeper are allowed to defend the penalty corner. No such limitation is placed on the numbers that the attacking team can employ. The problem that the defence must therefore solve is how to deploy five players to cover all the options available to the attack.

In general, the following patterns form the basis of most defending at penalty corners (*see* fig. 17).

● Player A in fig. 17 runs out to exert pressure on the striker. In so doing, his aim is to:
– hurry the striker into his shot and thereby force him possibly into a mistake, and/or to charge down the shot
– take a line that allows him to play the ball with the open stick, while covering any possibility of passes into other areas
– be prepared to slow down if it is obvious that the attackers are not going to strike the initial shot, or if the ball is passed to another striker
– be prepared to assist the other members of the defence in repelling subsequent phases of the attack.
● Player B runs to the right of player A, and slightly behind. It is his task to:
– cover and intercept any passes to attackers in and around the circle
– take the additional responsibility of

▲ *Fig. 17 Defending a penalty corner*

45

dealing with rebounds, knock-downs and other secondary phases of defence, whether off the goalkeeper or any other player

● Players C and D each have responsibility for the areas on either side of the goalkeeper and near to the goal posts.

● The goalkeeper usually takes up a position covering the middle parts of the goal, but in advance of players C and D. This position may be 2–7 yds off the goal line.

● Occasionally player D is deployed in a position alongside and to the left of the goalkeeper, from where he will be expected to cover any passes into an area to the left of and behind player A. Rebounds, knock-downs and deflections off and around the goalkeeper's left will also be his responsibility. This tactic may also help to catch advancing attackers in an offside position.

● Some goalkeepers come as far as possible off their goal line in order to narrow the angle of the shot and to exert pressure on the striker. But remember: the closer to the shot the goalkeeper is, the less time he has to react to it; the further off the goal line he is, the more vulnerable is the goal to shots from wide positions.

At set pieces such as these, the goalkeeper is the key defender. At all times he must be allowed a clear sight of the ball. He alone is equipped to deal effectively and safely with direct shots at goal.

Top class goalkeepers feel confident enough in their protective equipment and ability to use their entire bodies to smother and save shots at goal. This is an advanced skill and should **not** be attempted by the novice goalkeeper. The importance and value of using correct equipment and coaching methods, particularly with beginners and young players, cannot be over-stressed.

Questions

The pages on which the answers to these questions will be found are given in brackets.

(1) Is it permissible for a member of the team to change places with the goalkeeper? (page 3)
(2) Where must all players be for a pass-back (page 3)
(3) May a goalkeeper outside the circle kick the ball? (pages 5 and 17)
(4) How high should goal posts be? (page 5)
(5) May players wear metal badges and jewellery? (page 9)
(6) If the ball splits, how is the game restarted, and where? (page 11)
(7) When is the ball in play after a bully? (page 12)
(8) If the ball hits the goal posts and rebounds, should play go on? (page 12)
(9) May the ball be lifted at a push-in? (page 12)
(10) What happens when the ball passes over the back line off the stick of

an attacker? (page 12)

(11) May a player take a flying shot at goal following a hit from the back line? (page 14)

(12) May any player play or play at a ball above shoulder height? (page 14)

(13) Is it permissible to hit the ball with the rounded part of the stick? (page 16)

(14) May a player interfere with another player's stick? (page 16)

(15) A player accidentally kicks the ball – is this allowed? (page 16)

(16) Can a player be offside between the centre and the 25-yard line? (page 17)

(17) From where is a penalty corner taken? (page 22)

(18) Must the ball be stationary at a free hit? (page 24)

(19) Which part of the pitch should an umpire normally control? (page 25)

(20) Should extra time be allowed for penalty strokes? (page 25)

Metric conversion table

Imperial	Metric	Imperial	Metric
100 yards	91.4 metres	5 feet	1.5 metres
60 yards	54.9 metres	4 feet	1.2 metres
55 yards	50.2 metres	18 inches	45.7 centimetres
50 yards	45.7 metres	9.25 inches	23.5 centimetres
40 yards	36.6 metres	9 inches	22.9 centimetres
25 yards	22.9 metres	8.81 inches	22.4 centimetres
16 yards	14.6 metres	6 inches	15.2 centimetres
10 yards	9.1 metres	3 inches	7.6 centimetres
7 yards	6.4 metres	2 inches	5.1 centimetres
5 yards	4.6 metres	28 ounces	794 grams
4 yards	3.6 metres	12 ounces	340 grams
1 yard	1 metre	5.75 ounces	163 grams
7 feet	2.1 metres	5.5 ounces	156 grams

Index